*The*
*Connell Guide*
*to*

———————

# Christina Rossetti

———————

*by Anna Barton*

# Contents

### NOTES

# Introduction: Who is Christina Rossetti?

Christina Rossetti is one of the most significant and enduring poets of the 19th century. Best known as the author of intriguing, haunting and sometimes troubling lyric poetry, she published three collections of verse during her lifetime and contributed poetry to some of the most popular literary journals of the period. As well as poetry, she also published two collections of short stories, a collection of rhymes for children and six works of religious devotional literature.

Born in London in 1830, seven years before Queen Victoria ascended the throne, Christina was the youngest child of Gabriele Rossetti, an Italian immigrant who worked as a scholar and teacher of Italian, and Frances Polidori, the daughter of an Italian father and an English mother, who also worked as a teacher. She had three siblings: a sister, Maria, and two brothers, the editor and critic, William Michael and the artist and poet, Dante Gabriel. Her brothers were founding members of the Pre-Raphaelite Brotherhood, a loose association of artists and writers, who produced work that was both morally and stylistically controversial and hugely influential.

Rossetti did not marry and for most of her adult life she lived at home with her mother (her father died in 1854), her sister and her elder brother,

William Michael. It is therefore easy to make the mistake of viewing her life as one of domestic confinement and limitation. However, although Christina's family was not wealthy (indeed, Christina's work as a poet made a necessary contribution to the household finances), its connections to various cultural and scholarly networks and circles of influence meant that she lived her life in a rich literary and artistic environment where she was encouraged to develop and exert her creative talents. She had access to her father's extensive library; her grandfather paid for the publication of her first volume of poetry, *Verses: Dedicated to my Mother,* when she was just seventeen; and both her brothers encouraged her to contribute to their publishing endeavours.

Intertwined with the joint influences of literature and family, the other main source of authority and inspiration in Rossetti's life was her religious faith. She, her mother and her sister all attended Christ Church, Albany Street and were devotees of the Oxford Movement, which aimed to revive the Catholic tradition within Anglicanism.

Rossetti suffered from poor physical health and bouts of mental illness throughout her life. She died of breast cancer in 1894.

Although the facts of Christina's life are easy to come by, her identity and character remain somewhat mysterious to readers of her work, which does not reveal much about her opinions or emotions. Alison Chapman describes this quality of

Rossetti's poetry as a "resistance to inscribing the personal" and argues that it is a deliberate aspect of Rossetti's style, one that "dramatises both the impossibility of Victorian femininity and the impossibility of the woman poet caught within the sentimental tradition and the conflicted ideology of the Victorian literary marketplace". In other words, Rossetti avoids the personal in order to resist being reduced to a narrow, incomplete version of herself by a masculine literary tradition and a male-dominated marketplace.

Descriptions of Rossetti written by friends and family and Rossetti's own letters together present a sequence of contradictions that can be summed up by two pictures of Rossetti, both done by her brother, Dante Gabriel. The first, a pencil portrait done in 1866, represents the poet in a contemplative pose, her head resting on her hands, her hair tied neatly back from her face, looking into the middle distance (fig. 1)[*]. This is Christina as she was often memorialised: reserved, demure, studious and thoughtful.

The second, a private sketch that Dante sent to Christina in around 1865, is called "Christina Rossetti in a tantrum" and depicts the poet storming around her room, breaking mirrors, windows and furniture (fig. 2). The sketch is an affectionate joke that nevertheless gives us a glimpse of a different side to the poet's character, one whose extreme

[*]    See pages 21-22 for all figure images.

passion places the domestic tranquillity of her surroundings at risk. It is difficult to know which of the two sketches is the more accurate representation; but together they suggest the complexity of Rossetti's character as one that is not easily reduced to a particular stereotype of Victorian femininity.

# What is her poetry about?

In one sense, Rossetti's poetry is about all sorts of things. During her lifetime she wrote about love, death, social mores, religious faith, contemporary politics and the natural world. In another sense, however, it is often hard to grasp exactly what she is saying about any one of these topics. As a result, the reader can be left feeling wrong-footed or dissatisfied. In an early poem called "My Dream", a surreal fantasy featuring a fratricidal crocodile king, she suggests that the reason for this interpretive trickiness is that even she does not know what she means:

> *What can it mean? You ask. I answer not*
> *For meaning, but myself must echo, What?*
> *And tell it as I saw it on the spot.*

Rossetti's answer to a direct question from an imagined interlocutor about the meaning of her dream is ambiguous. She uses the line break to play with the transitive and intransitive meanings of "answer". At first it looks as though she is going to refuse to answer the question at all ("I answer not"). But then she seems to relent, as, reading across the line break, the phrase becomes, "I answer not / For meaning". But this is still a kind of non-answer, because it states that the poet cannot, or will not, take responsibility for the way her dream might be interpreted. She can, she says, only repeat the question back to the reader, giving interpretive responsibility over to us. Her role is to "tell it as I saw it", a phrase that implies openness and honesty, while actually giving nothing away. The poet protests her own ignorance and innocence; but the way she manipulates form and language in these lines suggests that she knows rather more than she is letting on.

Richard Cronin describes Rossetti's evasions as an "aesthetics of modesty", one that "finds its proper expression in the production of brief lyrics". A lyric can be briefly defined as the expression of a single idea or emotion as it happens. It often features an anonymous, first-person speaker, who addresses the reader directly and intimately. Sonnets are a kind of lyric, as are elegies; whereas narrative poems generally are not. When John Stuart Mill, writing in an essay entitled "What is poetry?" (1833), defined poetry as "feeling confessing itself to itself in moments of solitude", he was writing about lyric poetry. Likewise, when Wordsworth defined poetry as "the spontaneous overflow of powerful feeling" in his "Preface" to *Lyrical Ballads* (1802), it is lyric poetry that he has in mind. Lyric poetry became the focus of a new kind of critical attention in the 19th century. Because it was associated with emotional sincerity and direct expression, writers and critics saw lyric poetry as an opportunity to, quoting Wordsworth again, "see into the life of things" ("Lines written a few miles above Tintern Abbey") – to gain radical new perspectives on different aspects of individual and social life.

Rossetti's poetry both participates in and subverts this emergent tradition. Some of her most well-known poems are called "songs", underlining their association with lyric verse. Even more adopt its central characteristics: they are spoken in the first person and the speaker addresses us as if we were a close friend, or a lover ("my dearest", "my love"); they are brief and hold the promise of intensity and intimacy. Often, however, this promise remains unfulfilled and the speaker refuses to give herself, her thoughts and her feelings, away to her interlocutor. The look and sound of the lyric teases us with the expectation of connection, but the words of the poems work to keep the poet and her meaning hidden.

One of the best examples of Rossetti's subversive lyricism is "Winter: My Secret":

*I tell my secret? No indeed, not I;*
*Perhaps some day, who knows?*
*But not today; it froze, and blows and snows,*
*And you're too curious: fie!*
*You want to hear it? well:*

*Only, my secret's mine, and I won't tell.*

*Or, after all, perhaps there's none:*
*Suppose there is no secret after all,*
*But only just my fun.*
*Today's a nipping day, a biting day;*
*In which one wants a shawl,*
*A veil, a cloak, and other wraps:*
*I cannot ope to everyone who taps,*
*And let the draughts come whistling thro' my hall;*
*Come bounding and surrounding me,*
*Come buffeting, astounding me,*
*Nipping and clipping thro' my wraps and all.*
*I wear my mask for warmth: who ever shows*
*His nose to Russian snows*
*To be pecked at by every wind that blows?*
*You would not peck? I thank you for good will,*
*Believe, but leave the truth untested still.*

*Spring's an expansive time: yet I don't trust*
*March with its peck of dust,*
*Nor April with its rainbow-crowned brief showers,*
*Nor even May, whose flowers*
*One frost may wither thro' the sunless hours.*
*Perhaps some languid summer day,*
*When drowsy birds sing less and less,*
*And golden fruit is ripening to excess,*
*If there's not too much sun nor too much cloud,*
*And the warm wind is neither still nor loud,*
*Perhaps my secret I may say,*
*Or you may guess.* (1862)

This poem is both meta-lyric (a lyric about lyrics) and anti-lyric. It begins with a question that exposes the lyric reader's anticipation of some kind of private revelation. The speaker's (mock) affronted tone makes the reader feel nosey or intrusive, calling the value of lyric communication into doubt. But, after appearing to dismiss the possibility of interaction, the speaker keeps the reader hanging on with the suggestion of some future disclosure. She says that she might tell her secret "some day", but the poem seems to hold that day off, so that the more she talks, or writes, the further we get from the truth.

She even suggests that there may not be a secret at all, "But only just my fun". As such, she is an inversion of the conventional lyric speaker: fickle, insincere, untrustworthy and tight-lipped. Rather than revealing meaning, the poem encourages reflection on the act of reading and interpretation. It casts doubt on the ability of poetic language to express truth. The original title of this poem is "Nonsense", a title that more directly communicates the speaker's deliberate refusal to make sense. Deprived of a clear meaning, the reader is forced to look for a different way to engage with the text.

"Winter: My Secret" is a good introduction to Rossetti's poetry because, like much of her work, it refuses to reveal a simple answer. This is not the same as saying that her poems are meaningless. They are rich with suggestion and allusion that connects them to cultural, political and philo-sophical debates about gender, religion, politics and art. In "Winter: My Secret", for example, the title encourages the reader to consider the connection between secrecy and winter. Is winter a metaphor for something? The nature of her relationship with the reader, perhaps? Does it imply something broader about the human condition, or even about a world waiting for divine redemption?

The allusions to the speaker's body are especially interesting. The speaker compares divulging her secret to allowing access to her home and to her person, so that the search for the secret appears to be a kind of physical violation. Rossetti's secrecy therefore raises questions about the identity and role of the woman poet. We are encouraged to consider what might be at stake for a woman expressing herself in the way that the lyric tradition expects. By keeping her secret, the speaker also holds on to her power over the reader.

# Which writers influence her work?

The power that Rossetti wields over her reader is partly enabled by her confident engagement with a wide range of authors. She is a knowing participant in the traditions and conventions of women's poetry. Like many 19th-century poets (male and female), Rossetti was inspired by the archetypal poetess, the ancient Greek poet, Sappho. Sappho's works, only recovered as fragments, are a touchstone for a feminine tradition of spontaneous, emotionally charged, tragic love poetry. She is a powerful figure of feminine creativity; but her 19th-century reception risked reducing women's poetry to a matter of unmediated emotional outpouring, denying its intellectual and artistic potential.

Some of Rossetti's earliest poetry sees her negotiating Sappho's legacy and positioning herself alongside her more immediate female contemporaries. Her earliest collection includes a poem called "Sappho" (1847), in which the speaker desires that death put an end to her suffering and longs to be "Unconscious that none weep for me", expressing an interest in the relationship between the dead and the living that runs through much of her later poetry – for example, "After Death" and "Song (When I am Dead my Dearest)" (both 1862) – a connection which suggests that Rossetti's interest in death is not straightforwardly autobiographical, but is instead part of a performance of a certain kind of feminine artistry.

Reflecting on Rossetti's relationship with the Sapphic tradition, Yopie Prins writes that "in troping on the trope [of Sappho] she makes explicit a figural logic that has become the defining feature of women's sentimental lyric in the middle of the 19th century". In other words, Prins suggests that Rossetti's poetry self-consciously reflects on the way Sappho becomes a female "figure", endlessly re-imagined by poets and readers and thereby emptied of stable significance.

Rossetti also aligns herself with other female poets that she read and admired. Her first published collection includes a poem entitled "In the Round Tower at Jhansi, June 8, 1857", a poem that strongly resembles the work of late-Romantic poet, Felicia Hemans. Hemans's hugely popular collection, *Records of Women* (1828) reimagines historical and mythic narratives of female sacrifice and suffering. "In the Round Tower" takes up this theme, briefly recounting an apocryphal tale of a suicide pact between a British army captain and his wife, made during the Indian Mutiny.

The 1862 collection also includes "L.E.L." (1862), a tribute to the poet, Letitia Elizabeth Landon. Also writing within the Sapphic tradition, Landon's poetry, hugely popular in the early decades of the 19th century, frequently adopted the voice of the love-lorn female artist, whose artistic success is meagre compensation for romantic failure. Reflecting on the relationship between L.E.L. and Rossetti, Angela Leighton observes that Rossetti's poetry "takes the well-worn woman's pose 'to heart' but somehow emptie[s] it of all the cloying appeal of the earlier poet's verse, retaining only the shell, the exquisite formal shell of rhyme and metre".

"L.E.L.", which adopts this "pose", demonstrates Rossetti's keen understanding of L.E.L.'s manipulation of the role she plays in her poems. The speaker in Rossetti's poem expresses a suffering that isolates her from normal domestic life and from the creative cycles of the natural world:

> *Downstairs I laugh, I sport and jest with all:*
> *But in my solitary room above*
> *I turn my face in silence to the wall*
> *My heart is breaking for a little love.*
> *Though winter frosts are done,*
> *And birds pair every one,*
> *And leaves peep out, for springtide is begun.*

This isolation is sorrowful, but the reader is struck less by a sense of sorrow than by the beauty of the lines that describe it. The last quatrain demonstrates Rossetti's command of poetic metre; its perfect iambic rhythm creates a poise and harmony that perhaps feels more authentic than the speaker's hackneyed emotional state.

Rossetti's poem begins with an epigraph that is misattributed to a second 19th-century woman poet, Elizabeth Barrett Browning. Browning, who was one of the most successful poets of her day, also wrote a tribute to L.E.L., called "L.E.L.'s Last Question" and so, by naming Browning in her poem about Landon, Rossetti deliberately positions herself as the aspiring successor to the position of Britain's most celebrated female poet.

Elizabeth Barrett Browning's influence can be seen in Rossetti's experiments in the sonnet form, especially *Monna Innominata* (1881), a sequence of fourteen sonnets ("a sonnet of sonnets"), which, like Barrett Browning's *Sonnets from the Portuguese*

(1850), inverts the conventional Petrarchan set-up in which a male lover expresses his unrequited love to his silent female beloved. Like Barrett Browning, Rossetti gives the woman the speaking role and allows her to break free of the clichés of youth, purity and beauty that are perpetuated by a masculine poetic tradition. The final sonnet of the sequence imagines the female speaker in old age:

> *Youth gone and beauty gone, what doth remain?*
> *The longing of a heart pent up forlorn,*
> *A silent heart whose silence loves and longs;*
> *The silence of a heart which sang its songs.*

Like "Winter: My Secret", these lines play around with the idea of expression and withholding. Rossetti uses words to point towards a wordless realm that the reader cannot access. The power of silence for women's poetry is also something that Rossetti learns from Browning, who, in her own sonnet sequence, promises that she will love her beloved "in silence with thy soul" (Sonnet XXI).

Although Rossetti's poetry strongly identifies itself as part of a feminine poetic tradition, her influences range widely. Like her brothers, she was a great admirer of the late Romantic poet, John Keats, whose poetic exploration of melancholic states, of the desire for an escape from the mortal world into art or death and his belief in poetry as a space of self-negation (which he called "negative capability") all resonate with Rossetti's developing aesthetic.

She also took inspiration from Keats's narrative poems, which tell fantastic stories of doomed love. Keats's mythological register is employed in her best-known narrative poem, "Goblin Market" – which is discussed in depth at the end of this guide – and also in an early experiment in narrative poetry, "Repining" (first published in 1850). "Repining" rewrites Keats's poem, "The Eve of Saint Agnes", in which a young hero rescues his beloved from her oppressive family in the middle of the night. Rossetti's version tells the story of a young woman, who is rescued from a condition of isolated imprisonment by a mysterious "young man" who visits her at night.

However, whereas Keats's heroine is grateful for her rescue, which promises a happy ending in marriage, Rossetti's heroine is less fortunate. Her "rescuer" takes her to a sequence of different locations, which each show scenes of human terror and suffering. The poem ends with the woman pleading to be allowed to "return to whence I came". By choosing to return to seclusion and solitude rather than remaining in the mortal world, Rossetti's heroine reverses the ending of Keats's poem, forcing the reader to question the romantic fulfilment that Keats's poem celebrates.

As is typical of Rossetti's work, the "moral" of this choice is ambiguous. It is, perhaps, a choice of art over life: we first encounter the woman "spinning the weary thread away", an activity that is often associated with female creativity. But Rossetti also makes significant changes to the story that point towards the possibility of a religious interpretation. As Dinah Roe points out, her heroine, "rather than being awakened sexually, is awakened spiritually". The poem's hero is transformed from a lover into a Christ-like figure, whose entreaties – "rise up; be not afraid", "Rise, and follow me" – echo Jesus's words to his disciples (Matthew 9:9). "Repining" concludes without revealing whether the woman's plea for return is answered and so it becomes even more difficult to interpret Rossetti's attitude towards her story.

Rossetti's interrogation of Keatsian Romanticism situates her poetry alongside the work of other Victorian poets, notably Alfred Tennyson, whose early poems, "The Lady of Shallot" and "Mariana", also employ the figure of the embowered (isolated, secluded) woman in order to explore the relationship between art and life and to ask whether it might be possible to bridge the two. If the heroine of "Repining" is post-Keatsian, she is also Tennysonian. Her weaving connects her to "The Lady of Shallot" (1832), who "weaves by night and day" and the opening stanza of the poem, which describes the woman "spinning the weary thread away" and complaining, "Come, that I be no more alone", recalls the refrain of "Mariana" (1830):

*She only said, "My life is dreary,*
*He cometh not," she said;*

*She said, "I am aweary, aweary,*
*I would that I were dead!"*

In "The Lady of Shallot", the lady leaves her solitude, bringing down a curse that kills her; "Mariana" ends before any rescue takes place. Like Rossetti, Tennyson expresses a Victorian scepticism about the radical promise of Romanticism. Tennyson focuses on the experience of the female character in these tales of failed rescue and escape, a choice which suggests that for Victorian poets, male and female, femininity is a condition that expresses more than simply a woman's experience. Writing after Keats and Tennyson, Rossetti is able to use the feminine voice of her poetry to enter into artistic debates that move beyond gender to explore broader cultural questions. The female voice becomes a voice that resists (often in vain) the virile drive of Victorian progress.

Alongside these different poetic influences, Rossetti also took inspiration from writers of fiction. Her interest in dreamscapes, fantasy and the world beyond the grave draws on and combines a number of very diverse literary genres. The title of "The Prince's Progress", another narrative poem about a woman waiting for the arrival of her less than reliable prince, recalls John Bunyan's 17th-century narrative, *Pilgrim's Progress*, a textual echo that puts Rossetti's poetry into contact with a Christian allegorical tradition and provides an illuminating context for the mixture of biblical allusion and bizarre fairy-tale imagery that characterises a significant number of her poems and tales.

Rossetti builds on and subverts this tradition by combining it with a more modern genre, the gothic. From childhood onwards she was an avid reader of gothic texts. She especially enjoyed the work of Ann Radcliffe, whose novels, *The Mysteries of Udolpho* and *The Italian*, represent her father's native Italy as a place of adventure and feature a sequence of resourceful young heroines – prototypes, perhaps, for *Goblin Market*'s Lizzie and Laura. Rossetti's uncle, John Polidori was the author of a sensational gothic text, *The Vampyre,* and this family connection sheds potentially interesting light on all the "sucking" that takes place in *Goblin Market* and on the sonnet, "In an Artist's Studio", in which the speaker describes how the artist "feeds" upon his muse.

By injecting her poetry with the violence and fleshliness of the gothic, Rossetti upsets the relationship between the vehicle and the tenor (i.e. the metaphor and the message) in her work. Whereas in more straightforwardly allegorical literature, character and plot serve a clear interpretive purpose, in Rossetti's poetry humans and beasts alike exhibit a gothic intensity that grants them a life beyond their allegorical import. The desires, experiences and actions of the characters that populate Rossetti's narratives frequently take centre stage, refusing to map on to a clear intellectual pattern or structure and opening familiar moral questions up to new and unsettling scrutiny.

*Fig. 1: Portrait of Christina Rossetti, by her brother Dante Gabriel Rossetti (1866)*

*Fig. 2: "Christina Rossetti in a tantrum", (18*

*Fig. 3: "The Girldhood of Mary Virgin"*

*Fig. 4: "Ecce Ancilla Domini!"*

*Fig. 5 (above left): Dante's "Proserpine"*

*Fig. 6 (above right): "The Light of the World" by William Holman Hunt*

*Fig. 7 (below left): One of Dante's illustrations accompanying "Goblin Market" (1862)*

# FIVE FACTS ABOUT
## CHRISTINA ROSSETTI

**1.**

Rossetti is the author of the Christmas Carol, 'In the Bleak Midwinter'. It was first published in an American journal, *Scribner's Monthly*, in 1872.

**2.**

John Polidori, Rossetti's uncle, was a famous physician to Lord Byron and author of the first modern vampire tale, *The Vampyre* (1819).

**3.**

Rossetti was photographed by Charles Dodgson (a.k.a. Lewis Carroll), the author of *Alice's Adventures in Wonderland*, in 1863.

**4.**

Rossetti was one of the earliest anti-vivisection campaigners, believing that it was wrong to experiment on live animals.

**5.**

In 1973 *Playboy Magazine* published a series of illustrations inspired by Rossetti's most famous poem, *Goblin Market*.

# What is Rossetti's relationship to the Pre-Raphaelite Brotherhood?

The Pre-Raphaelite Brotherhood (PRB) was established by Dante Gabriel Rossetti in 1848. It was principally a collective of painters united by their dissatisfaction with the artistic establishment and with the teachings of the Royal Academy of Art, where Dante himself had been a student. The name that the group adopted refers to the Italian Renaissance painter, Raphael, whose work the Academy identified as its guiding example.

Dante Gabriel and his followers were determined to return to artistic principles that pre-dated Raphael and to break free of an art world they viewed as restrictive, hierarchical and overly professionalised. Perhaps because they were founded in a spirit of opposition, it is difficult to pin down the Pre-Raphaelite Brotherhood's own artistic principles. But their rejection of prevailing orthodoxies is associated with a return to nature and a celebration of inspiration over the dictates of reason. Their work often directs this naturalistic gaze to biblical narratives and other kinds of myth, attempting to find new truths in these familiar stories by viewing them with fresh eyes. An example of this aspect of their work is a painting by John Everett Millais called "Christ in the House of his

Parents" (1849-50), which, in its naturalistic representation of Christ as a small child in a carpenter's shop, was denounced by reviewers as blasphemous.

Anthony Harrison argues that "in a surprising number of ways the poetry of Christina Rossetti fits the avant-garde pattern that generally characterizes pre-raphaelite art and poetry". He draws a comparison between the way the PRB attacked the prevailing wisdom of the artistic establishment and the way Rossetti's poetry "provides a critique of the false values and premises of topical work by her contemporaries".

Rossetti was never a member of the brotherhood, however. Despite their radical principles, the PRB were less progressive when it came to matters of gender politics; and, when Dante Gabriel suggested that Christina be admitted as a member, Millais and William Holman Hunt (two other founding members) objected. In the end, Christina herself said she did not want to join the group and so her relationship to their artistic and literary activities remained peripheral. As a privileged observer of and occasional participant in their work, Rossetti produces poetry that both reflects and critiques Pre-Raphaelitism.

Along with the majority of women associated with the PRB, the most visible aspect of Christina's involvement was as an artist's model. Her poem, "In An Artist's Studio" (1896), reflects on the relationship between an artist and his muse:

*One face looks out from all his canvasses,*
*One selfsame figure sits or walks or leans;*
*We found her hidden just behind those screens,*
*That mirror gave back all her loveliness.*
*A queen in opal or in ruby dress,*
*A nameless girl in freshest summer greens,*
*A saint, an angel; – every canvass means*
*The same one meaning, neither more nor less.*
*He feeds upon her face by day and night,*
*And she with true kind eyes looks back on him*
*Fair as the moon and joyful as the light:*
*Not wan with waiting, not with sorrow dim;*
*Not as she is, but was when hope shone bright;*
*Not as she is, but as she fills his dream.*

As with her later sequence, *Monna Inominata*, Rossetti experiments with the Petrarchan tradition, using the artist and his model as stand-ins for the Petrarchan lover and his unattainable beloved and measuring them against the Petrarchan ideal, exposing it as bogus, or even dangerous.

The octet (the first eight lines) takes the reader on a tour of the studio. It employs repetition to emphasise the monotony that characterises the paintings it contains, which reduce its subject to "the same one meaning, neither more nor less". At the volta (the "turn" in a sonnet's argument that makes the transition from the octet to the sestet) the speaker introduces the artist, who has been absent up until this point. She writes that he "feeds" on the face of his model, employing a vampiric turn of phrase that introduces physicality and violence into the poem, intensifying the tone of Rossetti's critique.

"Feeds" is powerfully suggestive. It implies that the artist represents a threat to his model; but also that his relationship with her is one of dependency: he needs her to sustain himself. This sense of the artist's dependence complicates the power dynamics of the poem. The model appears to be the artist's victim; but at the same time she is granted a kind of subversive agency. She "looks back" at the artist, becoming the observer rather than an object to be observed; and, in the final line we are told that "she haunts his dream", so that it is she, as much as the vampire artist, who is invested with supernatural force.

The final lines suggest that the human woman represented in the pictures no longer looks the same as she does in the paintings. She is now "wan with waiting" (although we do not know what she is waiting for) and "with sorrow dim", so that again Rossetti appears to emphasise the cost of the interaction between artist and model. However, it is important to remember that Rossetti is a poet who is often more interested in dream worlds than in material existence. As a presence that haunts the dream of the artist, the model gains a power that exceeds the limits imposed on her by physical and social reality.

"In An Artist's Studio", which was written in 1856 (although it remained unpublished until after Rossetti's death), recalls her experience as a Pre-

Raphaelite muse. She was painted by a number of members of the brotherhood, most frequently by her brother, Dante Gabriel. The best known of his paintings that use Christina as a model are a pair that depict scenes from the life of the Virgin Mary: "The Girlhood of Mary Virgin" (fig. 3) and "Ecce Ancilla Domini!" (fig. 4) (which translates as, "Behold, the Handmaiden of the Lord!"), both of which represent scenes of submission and obedience.

"Ecce Ancilla Domini!" depicts the Annunciation (when the angel Gabriel informs Mary she is going to give birth to Christ). In this picture the angel stands over a vulnerable-looking Mary who crouches on her bed. In "The Girlhood of Mary Virgin", which Dante said represented "a symbol of female excellence", Mary sits in a room at a small table, doing needlework. Whereas other paintings depicting Mary's education show her engaged in reading, Dante decided that this was "an occupation obviously incompatible with these times" and so substituted the "more probable and at the same time less commonplace" activity of sewing for reading. If his decision is part of a bid for historical accuracy, it also suggests that his "ideal" woman is an illiterate one, a suggestion that presents obvious difficulties for his attitude towards his poet sister.

William Michael's note to "In An Artist's Studio" indicates that its more immediate inspiration was Dante's relationship with a second model, Elizabeth Siddall, whom he eventually married and whose troubled life was cut short in 1862 when she overdosed on laudanum. William's note draws attention to the fact that the speaker in the poem is neither artist nor muse, but a shadowy "we", who discloses nothing about herself except her perspective on the scene she describes. This introduction of a third party into the familiar binary dynamic of the sonnet captures something of Christina's relationship with the PRB: never taking up the role of either artist or model exclusively, she possessed a unique access to and understanding of each.

The PRB also offered Rossetti a route into publication. In 1850 the brotherhood launched a literary journal, *The Germ*, which was conceived as a means of disseminating the literary endeavours of the group. Rossetti had begun to publish poetry in journals and periodicals two years earlier and, encouraged by her brother, she contributed poems to each of the four issues in the journal's short run. These contributions are an important example of her brothers' involvement in her poetic career as editors and agents.

Christina frequently allowed her brothers to make editorial changes to her poems, to tweak her use of rhyme and metre so that it was more regular, and to alter the titles of her poems, exerting a kind of control over her published, professional identity that is perhaps not so different from the way D.G. Rossetti's paintings represented types of feminine identity that accorded with his ideals.

However, like the model described in "In An Artist's Studio", Rossetti's poetry does not submit easily to masculine interference. "Dream-Land", for example, the first of her poems to be published in *The Germ*, is a poem that represents a female figure idealised in the apparently passive condition of a sleep-like death. The poem appeared in the journal alongside a poem by Dante, called "My Sister's Sleep", which tells the story of an imaginary sister, Margaret, who dies in her sleep on Christmas Eve. Dante's "sleeping" sister resembles a statue on a tomb:

*The lids were shut; her uplaid arms*
*Covered her bosom.*

She is motionless and blind, and the action of the poem goes on around her. In "Dream-Land" the same conceit, of death as sleep, is handled very differently:

*Where sunless rivers weep*
*Their waves into the deep,*
*She sleeps a charmed sleep:*
  *Awake her not.*
*Led by a single star,*
*She came from very far*
*To seek where shadows are*
  *Her pleasant lot.*

*She left the rosy morn,*

*She left the fields of corn,*
*For twilight cold and lorn*
   *And water springs.*
*Through sleep, as through a veil,*
*She sees the sky look pale,*
*And hears the nightingale*
   *That sadly sings.*

Whereas "My Sister's Sleep" maintains a domestic focus, "Dream-Land" transports the reader to a kind of hinterland between death and life that resembles Xanadu, the fantastic location of Samuel Taylor Coleridge's famous dream-poem, "Kubla Khan":

*Where Alph the sacred river ran*
*Down to a sunless sea.*

This intertextual echo allows us to view Rossetti's dreamscape as a space of imaginative possibility. The second stanza, with its description of the female subject leaving "fields of corn / For twilight cold and lorn" alludes to the myth of Proserpine (later the subject of one of Dante Gabriel's most well-known paintings (fig. 5)), who was stolen from her mother, Ceres, goddess of agriculture, by Pluto, God of the underworld. Layered with literary allusion, Rossetti's dream-land is suggested as the creation of a powerful, authoritative imagination, not confined to the limits of feminine domesticity.

The liberation achieved in Rossetti's poem is

also reflected by its form. Whereas "My Sister's Sleep" employs an abba rhyme scheme, the a rhymes enclosing a central couplet in a way that reflects the kind of confined spaces that Dante's poem inhabits; "Dream-Land" employs an aaabcccb scheme, shortening the fourth and eighth line of each stanza to achieve a sense of openness or incompletion, a silent pause that hints at unspoken possibilities and insists that this dream-like death is not the end.

# Is Rossetti a feminist poet?

The strains of resistance that can be traced in Rossetti's work might be characterised as feminist. Within the macho environment of the Pre-Raphaelite Brotherhood, her poetry provides a counterbalance to the objectification and ideal-isation of women. In her life, she experienced a similar kind of counterbalance to fraternal influence via her involvement in a number of networks of female friendship and community that connected her to debates about women's rights and women's roles in mid-Victorian Britain.

Although the term "feminist" did not enter the language until the 1890s, the struggle for women's rights and women's suffrage gained momentum during the second half of the 19th century. Between 1850 and 1900 the laws governing marriage were gradually reformed, making it easier for women to divorce their husbands and allowing them to retain ownership of property after marriage. Rossetti's most direct connection to the women's rights movement was her association with the Langham Place circle, a group of middle-class women who worked to champion these aims. Just as she never joined the PRB, she was never a member of this radical group; but she met and corresponded with its members and entered into discussions with them about their radical cause.

Langham Place was the home of the *English Woman's Journal*, a feminist periodical founded by Barbara Leigh Smith (later Bodichon), Anna Jamieson, Bessie Parkes and Matilda Hays, which published radical political articles. In 1857, for example, the journal published "Women and Work", an article by Barbara Leigh Smith decrying the lack of professional opportunities available to women and arguing that "for two or three daughters to remain at home idle with the pretence of attending a father or mother... is absurd". These arguments were directly relevant to Rossetti's own situation. By remaining unmarried, Christina avoided the trap of coverture, which meant that anything earned or owned by a married woman belonged to her husband. But, working as a governess to help contribute to the family finances and having returned home to care for her dying father in 1854, she would have been aware both of the limited career options open to women and of the binding force of domestic duty.

The opening stanza of her poem, "From the Antique", also written in 1854, offers a bleak summary of a "woman's lot":

> It's a weary life, it is; she said: –
>   Double blank in a woman's lot
>     I wish and I wish I were a man;
>     Or, better than any being, were not...

The stanza echoes once again the world-weary refrain of Tennyson's Mariana; but Rossetti claims Mariana's weariness and her desire for obliteration for women in general. The title, "From the Antique", distances the woman in the poem from Rossetti herself by implying that the poem is a translation; but there is no known "antique" source for Rossetti's lyric and so the title appears to be an alibi, disguising a perspective that was closer to home than she wanted to admit.

At the same time, poems such as "No Thank you, John" (1862) offer a more spirited and playful response to a woman's prospects. In this poem, it is the male suitor who "waxes weariness", whereas the speaker shows herself to be more than capable of negotiating and subverting the language of courtship. Far from viewing both married and unmarried life as equally bleak prospects for women, "No Thank You, John" concludes with a cheerful offer of friendship, established on the speaker's own terms and not on those of her conventional and, we suspect, rather stupid, interlocutor.

The different attitudes Rossetti's poetry adopts towards gender politics reflect her complicated attitude towards "the woman question". Her letters demonstrate that she was in favour of allowing women to preach and to speak in parliament, but in 1871 she refused to sign a bill supporting women's suffrage, writing to Anna Jamieson that she had "no doubt that the highest functions are not in this world open to both sexes".

Her justification for this argument was theological. Rossetti reasoned that the Bible grants different roles to men and women, and that the same principle should apply in Victorian Britain. The complex interleaving of theological and political questions that informs her thinking about women's rights can be seen working themselves out in poems such as "The Lowest Room" (1875), which stages a conversation between two sisters: one who is content with a future as wife and mother, the other who rails against the limitations of a woman's life. At the end of the poem, the scene leaps forward 20 years and we learn that the first sister is married with a daughter and the second has become resigned to her unmarried state:

> So now in patience I possess
>     My soul year after tedious year,
> Content to take the lowest place,
>     The place assigned me here.

In the last two stanzas, this bitterness and

resignation is tempered by the speaker's faith:

> *Yet sometimes, when I feel my strength*
> *Most weak, and life most burdensome,*
> *I lift my eyes up to the hills*
> *From whence my help shall come:*

> *Yea, sometimes still I lift my heart*
> *To the Archangelic trumpet-burst,*
> *When all deep secrets shall be shown,*
> *And many last be first.*

These last stanzas are heavy with biblical allusion. The final line is taken from Jesus's words to his disciples, recorded in the Gospel of Matthew, "But many that are first shall be last; and the last shall be first" – words that promise the overturning of earthly hierarchies in heaven. The speaker lays claim to her place within a heavenly order that is more powerful than those patriarchal structures that refuse her access to the highest political and social functions. After 200 lines or so of anger, dissatisfaction and despair, however, these eight lines have to work quite hard to convince the modern reader that heavenly reward will make up for the material and intellectual restriction and restraint of a woman's experience.

Rossetti was also actively involved in a second network of women, the volunteers at the St Mary Magdalene Penitentiary in Highgate, who worked to rehabilitate young prostitutes. Prostitution had been brought to public attention as a social problem in 1858, when William Acton published a report entitled: "Prostitution considered in its Moral, Social and Sanitary Aspects, in London and other large cities: with Proposals for the Mitigation and Prevention of its Attendant Evils". The main public concern about prostitution was its contribution to the spread of venereal disease and so, in 1864, rather than outlawing prostitution, the government passed the Contagious Diseases Act, which empowered the authorities to subject any woman they suspected of being a prostitute to a medical examination and detain her for up to three months if she was found to be infected.

The obvious inequity of this Act, which did not allow the examination of male customers, meant that the prostitutes' cause was quickly taken up by the women's movement. Rossetti joined the Highgate Penitentiary as a volunteer in 1859 and worked there regularly, drawing on her experience as a teacher to instruct the inmates. There is no evidence that her work was motivated by political conviction, but she was nevertheless part of an institution that aimed to help rather than punish women who were often forced into prostitution by the lack of other available work.

Rossetti does not address the topic of prostitution directly in her poetry, but "Goblin Market", which she wrote in 1859, the same year she began work at Highgate, includes language and images that gesture towards the social and moral questions surrounding the subject. The final section of this guide has a more detailed reading of this, her most famous poem, which is by no means "just" about prostitution. Aspects of the work, however, are directly relevant to a discussion of the gender politics of her poetry.

The story of the poem centres around the fall of Laura, who is tempted to exchange a lock of her hair for a taste of goblin fruit. This fairy-tale transaction, of body for food, mirrors the exchange of sex for money made by a prostitute. The goblins, although not human, are described by Rossetti as "goblin men" and so the dynamics of the relationship between Laura and the goblins runs along gendered lines. The goblin fruit causes Laura to fall gravely ill, only to be saved by her sister, Lizzic. The poem concludes with Lizzie and Laura, now grown up, teaching their children that

> *"... there is no friend like a sister*
> *In calm or stormy weather:*
> *To cheer one on the tedious way,*
> *To fetch one if one goes astray,*
> *To lift one if one totters down,*
> *To strengthen whilst one stands."*

At Highgate, the volunteers were given the appellation "sister" and so "sister Christina's" poem tacitly celebrates the female community of volunteers and their charges. The poem was originally dedicated to Rossetti's actual sister, Maria, and so its last words express a layered appreciation of the different aspects of sisterhood, familial, artistic and charitable, that are crucial to her understanding of feminine identity.

Germaine Greer says that Christina Rossetti is, "if not a feminist poet, then a poet important for feminists", and it is true that, whatever her own complex attitude towards the question of women's rights, her work has been hugely important for feminist literary criticism from the second half of the 20th century onwards. Sandra Gilbert and Susan Gubar, in their groundbreaking feminist study of 19th-century women writers, *The Madwoman in the Attic*, first published in 1979, argue that Rossetti's poetry is an example of "an aesthetics of renunciation" and read her poetry as an attempt to make a virtue of the impotent condition that a patriarchal society thrusts upon her.

Whereas Gilbert and Gubar conclude that Rossetti's poetry is limited by this strategy, asserting that she "[buries] herself alive in a coffin of renunciation", later critics view her poetic style in a more positive light. Angela Leighton's influential work on Victorian women poets argues that she represents an attempt to subvert the idea that poetry by women dealt in emotional expression. One effect of this tradition was that it led to an understanding of women's writing as an extension of their bodies and therefore allowed it to be co-opted into a patriarchal ideology that viewed the woman as a material, bodily object rather than a thinking, speaking subject.

By writing, in Leighton's words, "against the heart", composing poems that are performances of emotional restraint, Rossetti's work is proposed by Leighton as a radical challenge to poetic orthodoxy. A third perspective is offered by Isobel Armstrong, who argues that she does not so much "obstruct" expression as play about with it, achieving a balance of expression and restraint that demonstrates her absolute mastery of her poetic materials.

These ideas enrich an understanding of Rossetti's engagement with the lyric tradition, and of her connections to other female poets. Alongside "Winter: My Secret", two lyrics that yield to this kind of feminist approach are Rossetti's poems, "Song" and "Remember" (1862):

### "Song"

*When I am dead, my dearest,*
*Sing no sad songs for me;*
*Plant thou no roses at my head,*
*Nor shady cypress tree:*
*Be the green grass above me*
*With showers and dewdrops wet;*
*And if thou wilt, remember,*
*And if thou wilt, forget.*

*I shall not see the shadows,*
*I shall not feel the rain;*
*I shall not hear the nightingale*

*Sing on, as if in pain:*
*And dreaming through the twilight*
*That doth not rise nor set,*
*Haply I may remember,*
*And haply may forget.*

### "Remember"

*Remember me when I am gone away,*
    *Gone far away into the silent land;*
    *When you can no more hold me by the hand,*
*Nor I half turn to go yet turning stay.*
*Remember me when no more day by day*
    *You tell me of our future that you plann'd:*
    *Only remember me; you understand*
*It will be late to counsel then or pray.*
*Yet if you should forget me for a while*
    *And afterwards remember, do not grieve:*
    *For if the darkness and corruption leave*
*A vestige of the thoughts that once I had,*
*Better by far you should forget and smile*
    *Than that you should remember and be sad.*

Like "The Lowest Room" and "Dream-Land", "Song" and "Remember" look forward to a posthumous existence, achieving a provocative balance between self-abnegation and assertion. Whereas poets often use their poems to preserve their memory, the speaker of "Song" implies that she does not care whether her "dearest" remembers or forgets her after she dies, a perspective that might suggest her sense of her own insignificance. The second stanza continues this work of obliteration with a description of the speaker's insensate body, which "haply" (meaning, here, "perhaps") will remember or forget her love.

At the same time it is impossible not to notice the assertive tone adopted by the speaker. The first stanza is made up of a list of commands with which she assumes full control of her afterlife. Her first instruction to her beloved, that he "sing no sad songs", contrasts playfully with the title of the poem, drawing attention to the fact that the speaker is singing while her beloved must remain silent. Likewise, in stanza two, the speaker's obliteration is achieved via three repetitions of "I shall not", which demonstrate a powerful and determined will that resists the annihilation that it also describes.

"Remember" begins more conventionally, though no less assertively, with a request for remembrance. But, as the sonnet progresses, it becomes clear that the speaker is offering her memory as a consolation to the person she is addressing rather than as part of a bid for her own posterity. Like "Song", "Remember" casts the afterlife as a negative space, one in which things are "not"; but in this second poem emphasis is placed on those aspects of the relationship between the speaker and her beloved that will end in death. When she is "gone away" her lover will not "hold" her, "tell" her, or "counsel" her. Bluntly put, he will no longer exert any control over her.

As in "Song", the sonnet's final lines speculate whether the speaker will hold on to her mortal thoughts after death and concludes that, if she does, it would be better that her beloved forget her. The logic that informs this reasoning is troubling. It suggests that the speaker's ghost will not desire to reconnect with her lover and implies that the speaker is eager that they go their separate ways. Both poems give us a female speaker who is not diminished in death, but is instead freed of those things that bind her to the mortal world and granted access to a wordless realm that her dearest and her readers cannot know.

# How does Rossetti's religious faith influence her writing?

Considering Rossetti's vexed attitude towards the woman question, it is possible to view her powerful religious faith as a constraining influence on both her life and her art. In poems like "The Lowest Room", female resignation and humility appear to be sanctioned by a patriarchal Christianity that condones obedience and self-denial.

Recent criticism, however, has begun to reassess the relationship between her faith and her art. Dinah Roe argues that while feminist scholarship has done much to revive the flagging poetic reputation of Rossetti, it has also established her in the modern imagination as a woman whose faith, gender, and creativity were incompatible impulses whose conflict made her miserable.

Roe thinks this approach "confuses the poetic *persona* with the poet, and overlooks the centrally important fact that making conflict into art is not a miserable act, but a redemptive one". In this respect, Rossetti's religious poetry can be compared to the poetry of the late-Victorian poet, Gerard Manley Hopkins, whose "Terrible Sonnets" stage similar kinds of redemptive conflict.

Roe describes the Bible as "easily Rossetti's greatest literary influence" and the poet's faith as her "inspiration" and her "muse". Certainly, the amount of devotional poetry and prose that she wrote during her lifetime and the extent to which she employs biblical language and imagery in her work suggest that her religious belief and her art were so closely intertwined that it is more accurate to understand her poetry as a kind of religious practice.

An example of this kind of devotional aesthetic is the poem, "A Birthday". This ecstatic lyric calls on a cornucopia of images to describe the speaker's feelings about her love, whose arrival is described, in the poem's final lines, as "the birthday of my life". The poem's rich imagery is drawn from the Old Testament text, The Song of Solomon, a lengthy praise-poem sung to God, whom it frequently compares to a lover. Rossetti's scripturally literate readership would therefore have recognised her "love" as God, or Christ, whose coming offers the possibility of rebirth and new life. "A Birthday" clearly demonstrates that, if her religion placed her work under certain constraints, those constraints must be understood as part of a system of belief that also sustained and inspired her.

This belief system was shaped by her involvement with the Oxford Movement and with Tractarianism. Between 1833 and 1841, the Oxford Movement, led by John Henry Newman, John Keble, Edward Pusey and William Manning, sought to revive kinds of worship that were associated with pre-Reformation England and had become alien to a modern Anglican tradition.

The introduction of these "High Church" or "Anglo-Catholic" rituals, such as the use of a sung liturgy, the wearing of priestly vestments and the re-introduction of confession, were controversial because they were seen as a threat to the fundamentals of British cultural identity. Tractarianism sprang out of The Oxford Movement and centred around the publication of *Tracts for the Times*, a sequence of 90 works that defended and promoted the Movement's ideas. As well as the Tracts themselves, Tractarianism prompted the publication of a variety of influential literary and theological works, including *The Christian Year* by John Keble, a sequence of poems written to aid devotion.

Christina's connection to the Oxford Movement came about via her attendance at Christ Church, Albany Street, the home of the Movement in London, which became an important social hub for Christina, her mother and her sister. (Rossetti's brothers gave up the church when they became independent, moving from religious scepticism to avowed atheism.) Kirstie Blair points out that, as part of the congregation at Christ Church, Rossetti became a "valued member" of "the intellectual and political elite"; and her devotional works often intercede directly and confidently on the urgent religious debates of the moment.

Her poetry can therefore be understood as part of a Tractarian poetic tradition. This context sheds a different light on the way her work withholds meaning and on its apparent reluctance to express feeling. These features both relate to the Tractarian doctrine of "reserve". Reserve was understood as a crucial aspect of Christian experience. The belief was that God's dealings with humankind involve the "holding back" of "sacred or important truths" that are beyond mortal comprehension – and that the natural world is a reserved expression of divinity. These ideas led to a focus on secrecy and mystery as aspects of religious language.

The doctrine also included an affirmation of emotional reserve and of poetic language as a controlled expression of an individual's spiritual and emotional life. These definitions of poetry complicate the connection between poetry and emotional sincerity that the Victorians inherited from the Romantics. They also help to explain the sometimes disconcerting experience of reading Rossetti's poetry: the apparently cool, detached tone of poems like "Song (When I am dead my dearest)" and the puzzling, contradictory imagery of "Goblin Market".

Tract 80, which sets out the doctrine of reserve, uses the parables as an example of narrative or literary reserve and argues that they are designed to "veil" rather than to clarify God's message. In other words, rather than telling his disciples the whole truth, Jesus's parables obscure that truth using illustrations from the mortal world that conceal and reveal at the same time. Rossetti's own devotional poetry often resembles the parables in this way. "Up-Hill" (1861) is a good example of her reserved aesthetic:

*Does the road wind up-hill all the way?*
   *Yes, to the very end.*
*Will the day's journey take the whole long day?*
   *From morn to night, my friend.*

*But is there for the night a resting-place?*
   *A roof for when the slow dark hours begin.*
*May not the darkness hide it from my face?*
   *You cannot miss that inn.*

*Shall I meet other wayfarers at night?*

*Those who have gone before.*
*Then must I knock, or call when just in sight?*
*They will not keep you standing at that door.*

*Shall I find comfort, travel-sore and weak?*
*Of labour you shall find the sum.*
*Will there be beds for me and all who seek?*
*Yea, beds for all who come.*

What is striking about this poem is that it is all
vehicle and no tenor, or all surface and no depth.
The conversation between the two speakers appears
to employ an up-hill journey as a metaphor for
Christian life. This is a familiar conceit, employed,
for example, by John Bunyan's *Pilgrim's Progress*.
The poem also employs a biblical lexicon. The
question, in stanza three – "Then must I knock, or
call when just in sight?" – recalls Matthew 7:7 in
which Jesus uses the same figurative language when
describing divine redemption to his disciples:
"knock and it shall be opened unto you" and the
words of Revelation 3:20, "Behold, I stand at the
door and knock; if any man hear My voice, and open
the door, I will come in to him, and will sup with
him, and he with Me" (these words also inspire
William Holman Hunt's painting, "The Light of the
World", which depicts Christ, holding a lantern,
standing with his hand poised to knock at a front
door (fig. 6)).

At the same time, unlike Matthew's gospel, and
unlike Hunt's painting, Rossetti's poem is

completely self-contained, giving no hint of its profounder meaning. It acts like the veil described in Tract 80. Its simple, often monosyllabic language and its reassuring but unforthcoming answers to the questions it asks, deliberately fail to get beyond the matter of the journey. As a result, the connection between these concrete concerns and the bigger, abstract questions of life, death and afterlife are left unexpressed, perhaps because they defy expression.

# Interpreting "Goblin Market"

"Goblin Market" is Rossetti's most famous work. Her brother, William, in his notes to his sister's poems, observes:

> I have more than once heard Christina say that she did not mean anything profound by this fairy tale – it is not a moral apologue consistently carried out in detail. Still the incidents are such as to be at any rate suggestive.

Writing an introduction to the poem three quarters of a century later, Germaine Greer says something similar:

> Now and then critics hint at what might be the

poem's theme, but more often they are content to let it lie enveloped in mystery, for fear that to unravel it would be to reveal more of the psychology of the unraveler than it would the meaning of the poem.

Like so many of Rossetti's poems, "Goblin Market" both invites and defies analysis. Its story of temptation and salvation opens up a range of interpretive possibilities and raise a number of different political, theological and moral questions. As her brother says, however, the poem does not deal consistently with any one of these. Its plot, language and form often pull the perspective of the poem in different directions, and it brings together many of the themes already explored in this guide, playing them off one another and insisting that neither politics, religion or art can be considered in isolation.

## What story does the poem tell?

"Goblin Market" tells the story of two sisters, Lizzie and Laura, who are tempted to taste the exotic fruit sold by a troop of goblin men. Lizzie warns Laura that they must not "peep at goblin men"; but Laura ignores her warnings. Left alone by Lizzie, Laura is approached by the goblins and, because she has no money, she exchanges a lock of her hair for some fruit. She feasts and then returns home where she is scolded by Lizzie, who reminds her of the fate of

Jeanie, another girl, who died after tasting the goblin fruit. Laura is unconcerned at first; but later she is distressed to find that she can no longer hear the cry of the goblins and she begins to pine away.

Remembering Jeanie, Lizzie decides to act and goes in search of the goblins. She attempts to buy fruit to take home to her sister, but the goblins refuse her money and ask her to sit and eat with them instead. Lizzie refuses and the goblins attack her, attempting to force the fruit into her mouth. She resists and returns home bruised and covered in fruit juice, which her sister kisses from her body. This time the fruit is repulsive to Laura and causes her to fall into a fit. She subsequently recovers and the poem concludes with a description of the two sisters, years later, married and with daughters of their own.

## When did Rossetti write "Goblin Market"?

She wrote it in 1859, while working at the Highgate Penitentiary. It was first published in 1862. There are some notable differences between her manuscript and the published poem, the most significant being the title. The poem was originally called "A Peep at the Goblins", a title that acknowledges the influence of *A Peep at the Pixies* (1854), a collection of fairy tales by her cousin, Anne Eliza Bray. The published title, suggested by Dante Gabriel Rossetti, replaces this intertextual reference and steers the reader's attention away from the curiosity that motivates the two sisters and on to questions of buying and selling. She illustrated her original manuscript with sketches that are replaced in the published text by a set of woodcuts, also by her brother, Dante (fig. 7).

## What makes the poem so distinctive?

"Goblin Market" employs an uneven metre and irregular rhyme scheme. The lines are of varying lengths and linked together with a mixture of rhyming couplets, abab rhymes and unrhymed lines. Dante sent the manuscript of the poem to his friend, the critic, John Ruskin, who replied saying the poem's "irregular measures" were a "calamity of modern poetry" and advising Rossetti to write more disciplined verse. This dismissal of the peculiar form of "Goblin Market" as bad writing ignores the powerful, unruly energy it generates. In the opening lines, for example, we experience a breakdown of regular form as the voice of the goblins is introduced:

*Morning and evening*
*Maids heard the goblins cry:*
*"Come buy our orchard fruits,*
*Come buy, come buy:*
*Apples and quinces,*
*Lemons and oranges,*
*Plump unpecked cherries,*
*Melons and raspberries,*

*Bloom-down-cheeked peaches,*
*Swart-headed mulberries,*
*Wild free-born cranberries,*
*Crab-apples, dewberries,*
*Pine apples, blackberries;*
*Apricots strawberries; —*
*All ripe together*

The first four lines are restrained and fairly regular: Two trimeter (three-stress) lines are enclosed within two dimeter (two-stress) lines and the rhyme scheme appears to set up an abab pattern. But the extraordinary list of produce described by the goblins creates an intoxicating rhythmic momentum, so that the feel and sound of the poem participates in the temptation that it describes, allowing the reader to experience the sensual attraction of the goblin fruit.

The alignment of language and fruit as two kinds of sensual experience complicates the moral scheme of the poem. Perhaps the reader should be suspicious of the aesthetic pleasure provided by the verse; or perhaps the pleasure offered by the goblins' fruit is not straightforwardly bad. The "calamitous" form of the poem encourages this kind of interpretive nuance and destabilises the relationship between the reader and the story.

## Who, or what, are the goblins?

They are referred to as "goblins", "goblin men" and

"merchant men" and described as fantastic, hybrid creatures, each one characterised by a different animal characteristic, looking or moving like a "cat", a "snail", a "wombat", or a "ratel". This suggests that the threat represented by the goblins is multiple. Their association with fairy-tales and the supernatural contrasts with Lizzie and Laura, who occupy a recognisably human realm, and connects the goblins to the world of the imagination, encouraging the reader to consider the temptations and dangers of that world.

This is the perspective explored by Gilbert and Gubar, who write that the goblins represent "the desirous creatures so many women have recorded encountering in the haunted glens of their own minds", and suggest that the fruit they sell is the "unnatural, but honey-sweet fruit that is analogous to (or identical with) the luscious fruit of self-gratifying pleasure".

At the same time, the fact that they are "men" invites a gendered reading of the poem, suggesting Laura and Lizzie as the female victims of patriarchal exploitation, violence and control. "Merchant men" connects them to the marketplace, inviting consideration of the poem's attitude towards trade, capitalist economics and consumerism. The connection Rossetti draws between the goblins and the animal kingdom, especially the references to wombats and ratels (a kind of badger, native to Africa and parts of Asia), draws on her encounters with the exotic beasts at London Zoo and positions the poem within the context of contemporary scientific discoveries (Darwin's *On the Origin of Species* was published in the same year as the poem's composition) and the expansion of the British Empire.

## What is the significance of the fruit?

Within a Judeo-Christian tradition, fruit is associated with temptation and sin. In Genesis, Eve is tempted by the serpent to eat fruit from the Tree of the Knowledge of Good and Evil. Doing so, she disobeys God's instructions and causes humanity's fall from grace. This "fall" into knowledge is often associated with the loss of sexual innocence, an interpretation that is also encouraged by the descriptions of Laura's physical appetite for and sensuous enjoyment of the fruit.

At the same time, the temptation that the fruit represents is not straightforwardly carnal. It also represents the attraction of enlightenment and the temptation of disobedience. The poem is certainly ambivalent about Laura's desire to see and hear the goblins, which, in contrast to Lizzie's strict observance of the rules, appears both natural and beautiful:

> *Laura stretched her gleaming neck*
> *Like a rush-imbedded swan,*
> *Like a lily from the beck,*
> *Like a moonlit poplar branch*

*Like a vessel at the launch*
*When its last restraint is gone.*

This list of similes creates a sense of pastoral tranquility and complicates our attitude to Laura's impulses and appetites. The images suggest they are misdirected or abused because of her encounter with the goblins.

## Who is Jeanie?

The story of Jeanie, which acts as a warning to Lizzie and foreshadows Laura's actions and their consequences, is a story within a story that alerts the reader to the capacity of storytelling (and also, therefore, of poetry) to be a source of communal knowledge and shared experience. Jeanie's name points towards a second, more specific, interpretive context: "Jeanie" recalls "Jenny", the title of a poem by Dante Gabriel Rossetti, composed between 1848 and 1859, which describes an encounter between a male speaker and a prostitute. This intertextual allusion implies a connection between the trade Laura makes with the goblins and the exchange between prostitute and customer and acts as a subtle counter to the masculine perspective provided by Christina's brother's poem.

## How does Lizzie save her sister?

If Laura is like Eve, then Lizzie's actions align her

with Christ. She saves her sister by sacrificing herself. The description of the goblins' attack is graphic and febrile, and their physical violence is described in terms that imply sexual aggression, too. The goblins kiss, squeeze and caress her and then attempt to force their fruit into her mouth, to "open lip from lip", a phrase with clear gynaecological overtones. While she endures the goblins' attack, Lizzie is described in terms that emphasise her absolute purity:

*White and golden Lizzie stood,*
*Like a lily in a flood, –*
*Like a rock of blue-veined stone*
*Lashed by tides obstreperously, –*
*Like a beacon left alone*
*In a hoary roaring sea,*
*Sending up a golden fire, –*

This list of similes emphasises Lizzie's impenetrability and paints her white, golden and blue, colours emblematic of the Virgin Mary. The lines also echo the description of Laura when she first peeps at the goblins, creating one of the poem's many suggestive parallels and repetitions.

When Lizzie returns to Laura she addresses her sister using words that again combine Christian symbolism with sexual imagery:

*She cried "Laura" up the garden,*
*"Did you miss me?*

*Come and kiss me.*
*Never mind my bruises,*
*Hug me kiss me, suck my juices*
*Squeezed from goblin fruits for you,*
*Goblin pulp and goblin dew.*
*Eat me, drink me, love me;"*

The phrase "eat me, drink me" recalls the words of the Communion service in which participants eat and drink the body and blood of Christ, which are represented by bread and wine. By inviting her sister to hug and kiss her, Lizzie asks Laura to repeat the actions of the goblins. By inviting her to "suck my juices", Lizzie appears to transform her body itself into a kind of fruit that might satisfy her sister's appetite.

Margaret Homans puts it nicely when she writes, "having been reduced to mere body... by the goblins' assault, Lizzie experiences that body as a source of power" (p.589). This elision of homo-eroticism and salvation is one of those aspects of the poem that is not fully or consistently developed. The sisters end the poem married and with children. Nevertheless, the moment of intense physical encounter between the sisters remains to trouble the hetero-normative conclusion of the tale.

Whether or not the poem's sexual sub-text is acknowledged, the poem's last lines, which instruct the reader that "there is no friend like a sister" offer what Jerome McGann describes as "an alternative, uncorrupted mode of social relation – the love of sisters" – that might replace, or at least counteract, the commercial, patriarchal relationships that underpin Victorian society.

# Conclusion: why read Rossetti?

In 1928 Virginia Woolf, the modernist author and critic, named Rossetti in her seminal work of feminist literary criticism, *A Room of One's Own*. Woolf derided her as an example of a Victorian literary tradition that had been exposed as naïve by the devastating realities of World War One, and implied that her work had become irrelevant to a disillusioned, post-War world: "the illusion which inspired [...] Christina Rossetti to sing passionately about the coming of [her] love is far rarer now than then".

Two years later, however, in a short essay, entitled "I am Christina Rossetti", Woolf re-evaluated the poet, this time finding in her work qualities that survive beyond the perceived limitations of her Victorian context:

> Modest though you were still you were drastic, sure of your gift, convinced of your vision... In a word, you were an artist.

These two contrasting accounts of Rossetti mark

the starting point of her 20th-century critical heritage, and together capture something of her continuing significance. Her poetry is important because it reflects and critiques some of the major intellectual, political and cultural trends of Victorian times; but its drastic vision is also one that can speak to us directly, inviting us to participate in its provocations and pleasures.

## SELECTED BIBLIOGRAPY

Isobel Armstrong, *Victorian Poetry: Poetry Poetics, Politics* (Oxford: Blackwell, 1993).

Kirstie Blair, *Form and Faith in Victorian Poetry and Religion* (Oxford: Oxford University Press, 2010)

Alison Chapman, *The Afterlife of Christina Rossetti* (Basingstoke: Palgrave, 2000)

Richard Cronin, *Reading Victorian Poetry* (Oxford: Wiley-Blackwell, 2011)

W.E. Freedman (ed.), *The Correspondence of Dante Gabriel Rossetti*, 10 vols. (Cambridge: D.S. Brewer, 2002-2015).

Germaine Greer, *Slipshod Sibyls:* Recognition, Rejection and the Woman Poet (New York: Viking, 1995)

Jan Marsh, *Christina Rossetti: A Literary Biography* (London: Pimlico, 1995).

John Stuart Mill, "Thoughts on Poetry and its Varieties", *The Monthly Repository* (1833).

Sandra Gilbert and Susan Gubar, *The Madwoman in the Attic: The Woman Writer in the 19th-Century Literary Imagination* (New Haven: Yale University Press, 1979).

Anthony H. Harrison, *Christina Rossetti in Context* (Chapel Hill: University of North Carolina Press, 1988).

Margaret Homans, "'Syllables of Velvet': Dickinson, Rossetti and the Rhetoric of Sexuality", *Feminist Studies* 11.3 (1988), pp. 569-593.

Jerome McGann, "Christina Rossetti's poems: a new edition and a revalutation", *Victorian Studies* 23 (1980), pp. 237-254.

Yopie Prins, *Victorian Sappho* (Princeton, New Jersey: Princeton University Press, 1999)

Dinah Roe, *Christina Rossetti's Faithful Imagination* (Basingstoke: Palgrave, 2006)

Christina Rossetti, *The Complete Poems of Christina*

*Rossetti: A Variorum Edition*, ed. R.W. Crump, 3 vols (Louisiana: Louisiana State University Press, 1979-90).

William Michael Rossetti, "Memoir", in *The Poetical Works of Christina Rossetti* (London: Macmillan, 1904).

Angela Leighton, *Victorian Women Poets: Writing Against the Heart* (London: Harvester Wheatsheaf, 1992).

Virginia Woolf, "I am Christina Rossetti", *The Second Common Reader* [1932] (New York: Harcourt, 1960), pp. 214-221.

Virginia Woolf, *A Room of One's Own* [1928], (Harmondsworth: Penguin, 1945).

William Wordsworth, "Preface" to *The Lyrical Ballads* [1802], Stephen Gill (ed.), *William Wordsworth: The Major Works* (Oxford: Oxford University Press, 1984), pp. 595-616.

William Wordsworth, "Lines written a few miles above Tintern Abbey", *The Major Works*, p. 130.

www.rossettiarchive.org

# ⑥G CONNELL GUIDES

*Concise, intelligent guides to history and literature*

---

## CONNELL GUIDES TO LITERATURE

**Novels and poetry**
*Emma*
*Far From the Madding Crowd*
*Frankenstein*
*Great Expectations*
*Hard Times*
*Heart of Darkness*
*Jane Eyre*
*Lord of the Flies*
*Mansfield Park*
*Middlemarch*
*Mrs Dalloway*
*Paradise Lost*
*Persuasion*
*Pride and Prejudice*
*Tess of the D'Urbervilles*
*The Canterbury Tales*
*The Great Gatsby*
*The Poetry of Robert Browning*
*The Waste Land*
*To Kill A Mockingbird*
*Wuthering Heights*

**Shakespeare**
*A Midsummer Night's Dream*
*Antony and Cleopatra*
*Hamlet*
*Julius Caesar*

*King Lear*
*Macbeth*
*Othello*
*Romeo and Juliet*
*The Second Tetralogy*
*The Tempest*
*Twelfth Night*

**Modern texts**
*A Doll's House*
*A Room with a View*
*A Streetcar Named Desire*
*An Inspector Calls*
*Animal Farm*
*Atonement*
*Beloved*
*Birdsong*
*Hullabaloo*
*Never Let Me Go*
*Of Mice and Men*
*Rebecca*
*Spies*
*The Bloody Chamber*
*The Catcher in the Rye*
*The History Boys*
*The Road*
*Vernon God Little*
*Waiting for Godot*

NEW

| | |
|---|---|
| American Literature | How to Write Well |
| Dystopian Literature | The Gothic |
| How to Read a Poem | The Poetry of Christina Rossetti |
| How to Read Shakespeare | Women in Literature |

---

## NEW: CONNELL GUIDES TO HISTORY

**Guides**
The French Revolution
Winston Churchill
World War One
The Rise and Fall of the Third Reich
The American Civil War
Stalin
Lenin
Nelson
The Tudors
Napoleon

The Cold War
The American Civil Rights Movement
The Normans
Russia and its Rulers

**Short Guides**
Britain after World War Two
Edward VI
Mary I
The General Strike
The Suffragettes

---

*"Connell Guides should be required reading in every school in the country."*
**Julian Fellowes, creator of Downton Abbey**

*"What Connell Guides do is bring immediacy and clarity: brevity with depth. They unlock the complex and offer students an entry route."*
**Colin Hall, Head of Holland Park School**

*"These guides are a godsend. I'm so glad I found them."*
**Jessica Enthoven, A Level student, St Mary's Calne**

---

To buy any of these guides, or for more information, go to
**www.connellguides.com**
or contact us on (020)79932644 / info@connellguides.com

First published in 2017 by
Connell Guides
Spye Arch House
Spye Park
Lacock
Wiltshire
SN15 2PR

10 9 8 7 6 5 4 3 2 1

A CIP catalogue record for this book is available from the British Library.
ISBN 978-1-911187-61-5

Design © Nathan Burton
Assistant Editor:
Paul Woodward

Printed in Great Britain

www.connellguides.com